Republican Motherhood: A Disquisition on Life, Liberty, and the Pursuit of Happiness

While every precaution has been taken in the preparation of this book, the publisher assumes no responsibility for errors or omissions, or for damages resulting from the use of the information contained herein.

REPUBLICAN MOTHERHOOD: A DISQUISITION ON LIFE, LIBERTY, AND THE PURSUIT OF HAPPINESS

First edition. October 14, 2024.

Copyright © 2024 Dr. Amanda Wiles.

ISBN: 979-8227150868

Written by Dr. Amanda Wiles.

Also by Dr. Amanda Wiles

Daughter of the Mountain
Heart of the Mountain

From Hells to Hollis
The Magi's Madame
The Assassin's Angel

Standalone
The Mad Science of HR
Republican Motherhood: A Disquisition on Life, Liberty, and
the Pursuit of Happiness

Table of Contents

Dramatis Personae

The Nuclear Family

I/Me - Known by many names–Mom, Sister, Babe–and almost never called Amanda. I write books, play games, and love to eat.

Hubs - My wonderful, supportive husband, 'Papi' to our children, and beloved Game Master of our Tabletop Gaming Family

Mon Fills (French for "My son") - My oldest son and proud pre-tween, he has all the bravado of a seventeen-year-old and all the anxiety of an introverted thirty-year-old. He's learning French at school and Korean in martial arts.

Mijo (Spanish for "My son") - My youngest son and wild daredevil, he wants to run fast and eat cucumbers like popsicles. He's learning Spanish at school and likes to show off in front of a crowd.

The Village

Mommo & Daddo - My mom and dad.

Smithy, Stabby, Squire, Grandar, Macaroni, Dex, First Wife, New Girl - Our gaming family.

The Girls (Dutchess, Joylyn, Expat) - My best

friends since high school.

Great American Bean Pole & Betty Boop - My nephew and niece.

Cyclops - The second of my three older brothers, father of the Great American Bean Pole and Betty Boop.

G6 - All the grandparents our kids are blessed to have.

Third Mom - My dear friend, the boys' bonus mom, and mother of my bonus daughter.

Our Community - Countless people who have been in and out of our lives over the years. They've each made our lives better, more interesting, and more filled with love. Friends, teachers, coworkers, and even the manager of a Walmart Auto Center in the middle of nowhere Louisiana who fixed our flat tire even though the auto section closed five minutes before we got there.

This book is dedicated to all the amazing young people in our chosen family and community–Mia, Brayden, Ethen, Delilah, Mason, Jyn, Revan, Adeline, Bodie, and so many others–I can't wait to see the amazing things you accomplish in this world!

Prologue - My Declaration of Independence

"The genius of republican liberty seems to demand on one side, not only that all power should be derived from the people, but that those entrusted with it should be kept in independence on the people, by a short duration of their appointments; and that even during this short period the trust should be placed not in a few, but a number of hands."

- James Madison, Federalist Papers No. 39

First and foremost, I must state up front: I am NOT, nor have I ever been, a registered Republican. I don't think I've ever registered as a Democrat, either, but I have no idea where to check. To the best of my recollection, I registered as an Independent when I was 18 and haven't changed it since. In the interest of transparency, I will tell you I have voted Democrat in every election since.

The title of this book doesn't refer to my political preferences or have anything to do with raising young Republicans. The title references a Revolutionary War era ideology of how women contribute to our nation.

Republican Motherhood emphasized the importance of women's roles as wives and mothers in national politics...sort of.

However the ideology was originally intended, the message that trickled down to me from my elementary school textbook was this: the most important thing a woman can do to 'participate' in politics and shape the future of the nation is to raise and educate her children.

When I read the little paragraph in Mrs. C's 6th grade social studies class, I remember looking at the pencil drawing of a colonial woman and being uncomfortable, though I didn't understand why. Conscious thoughts of motherhood had yet to form in my imagination, though I had the standard compliment of baby dolls and caregiver training toys.

It was the autumn of 2000 and the presidential election was top of the hour for news shows and top headlines for newspapers. As a twelve-year-old girl growing up in the deeply red state of Oklahoma, it was a stressful time for me.

My mom, Mommo, was the only person, man or woman, I knew of supporting Al Gore, the Democratic presidential candidate. Literally all the other adults in my life were staunch supporters of George W. Bush.

The REPUBLICAN candidate.

In my adolescent mind, I linked the concept of Republican Motherhood with the Republican political party. A misunderstanding that was only strengthened by the community I grew up in, the media I had access to, and the composition of national politics at the time.

Women, while allowed to work, were not present in large numbers in the halls of government, the boardrooms of companies, or the typical protagonists of TV shows—at least not the ones watched in my household.

All of these influences and subconscious lessons were in dissonance with the force of nature that was and *is* my mom. She was an oddity, an outlier. She worked full time in oil and gas, managed our household of four kids, and was an elected official on the local school board. To my adolescent mind, she was the antithesis of Republican Motherhood.

At twelve, I understood my mom was different. I wanted to be like her, I didn't want to stay in the box of wife and mother. But I also understood being different was hard and I'm not the stone-solid, outspoken warrior she is.

As I grew older, I learned other terms and concepts around a woman's role in our society, like Women's Rights, Equal Pay for Equal Work, and the Right to Choose. The more I learned, the more angry I became about the idea of Republican Motherhood.

What's between my ears is more important than what's between my legs!

I was furious! I would be different! I was going to fight back against The System! Or The Man! Or...whatever!

And fight back I did, the only way I knew how: quietly and unobtrusively. I'm a naturally non-confrontational person, usually acting as a peacemaker in conflict.

Someone get a guitar and start playing Kumbaya so we can make our friendship bracelets!

That's more my speed.

My way of fighting back was to get my bachelor's, master's, and doctorate degrees while working full time in human resources and building a life with my husband, Hubs.

I didn't have kids yet. There was an undefinable point in the future when Hubs and I agreed we would talk about starting a family. He wanted to be out of the Navy and I wanted to finish my bachelors and then my master's degree.

He was honorably discharged in 2011 and we moved home. Hubs started working for the VA. I finished one degree and moved on to the next while I worked my way into progressively more challenging jobs.

Still, we weren't ready for kids.

I was a childless cat AND dog lady (two of each), but I could still make a difference in my own way. I chose to be different with kindness, positivity, and genuine connection with the people I came across in life.

Not everyone appreciated my brand of rebelliousness; I was once called "relentlessly cheerful". It was **not** a compliment. Yet it was a sign I was making a difference!

I saw a quote the other day that summed up my philosophy of fighting back perfectly. Nobel Peace Prize winner Desmond Tutu said: "Do your little bit of good where you are; it's those little bits of good put together that overwhelm the world."

In the places and spaces where I've been, I've tried to do a little bit of good. I haven't overwhelmed the world yet, but I was making a difference in people's lives long before I became a mother–and I almost wasn't a mother at all.

Hubs and I married young–too young, truth be told– but we were constantly asked when we were going to have children. All the female relatives in our support system seemed to be counting down the minutes until I made THE announcement.

Except Mommo. Again the rebel, the oddity, the mold breaker.

It took nearly a decade for my husband and I to decide to start trying. It took several more years to find out I can't get pregnant.

Hearing that news was…overwhelming. And terrifying. Suddenly the passage from my 6th grade social studies book loomed large in my psyche.

The deeply ingrained idea my value and worth was intrinsically tied to my vagina and womb made accepting my infertile reality extremely difficult. The internalized shame ran deep in my core and made it hard to tell anyone, effectively isolating Hubs and I from the love and support of the people around us.

Then I remembered Mommo's consistent disregard for the 'normal', for the 'traditional' role of a woman in family, work, and citizenship.

Slowly, I marshaled the courage to tell her.

Just her. No one else. Not Hubs' mother, not our friends. Just my mom. I felt broken and vulnerable, so I didn't *want* anyone else to know.

It was April of 2020. The world was frozen in peril, the pandemic just beginning to ravage our families and communities. I worked in an 'essential' industry, so I had a letter giving me permission to break the quarantine.

Driving home from work, I was the only car on the road, with miles of pavement in front of and behind me, miles of farmland stretching out on either side of me.

All alone on the road and on an emotional island of my own making.

Mommo called. I was expecting it. It was my 31st birthday. I'd already had calls and texts from so many lovely people in my life.

But Mommo knew I had a long commute (an hour and a half) so she waited to call me until I was driving, so we could have a nice long chat. Once we'd run through the birthday wishes, the events of the day, the family news, and all our other normal topics, I finally just told her.

"Hubs and I have been trying for kids but the doctor says I can't get pregnant."

If I hadn't been driving, I probably would have buried my head in my hands. For a moment, there was silence.

Then, because Mommo never does what one would expect, her very first response took me off guard, "Have you and Hubs considered adopting? I had lunch with my friend the other day and they are looking for a family to adopt their 18-month-old grandson."

A week later, I met her friend. A few weeks later, Hubs and I met our first son, Mijo, on Mother's Day of 2020. Now, four years later, we have a second son, Mon Fills, as well.

I'm a mom.

A hot mess express.

But also a mom.

With unbelievable luck and grace, the universe granted me the chance to quietly and unobtrusively rebel against the idea of Republican Motherhood one last time: by raising my kids to reject the very principle itself.

Except...I don't want to...

The idea of Republican Motherhood has taken root but not in the way it did back when I was twelve. I realize now, I have the ability and responsibility to teach my children how to be good human beings. I still contribute to the world in my own way, but I *increase* my contribution by raising my kids to be decent and caring people.

I have a goal! I have a mission!

I have...no idea what I'm doing.

Most parents grow in parenthood as their children grow older. We jumped into parenthood at the 2-year-old mark and then a few years later, skipped ahead with our oldest to the 11-year-old mark.

We are frantically laying down the railroad tracks a few feet in front of this parenting train. Facing decisions like cell phones and web access along with conversations about sex and puberty while simultaneously learning how to teach reading, personal hygiene, and safe interaction with animals.

Hot. Mess. Express.

But I am doggedly determined to apply MY brand of Republican Motherhood to this runaway locomotive–heavy emphasis on the 'LOCO'.

Safe, Loved, and a Little Bit Crazy

When I started this book, I wanted to talk about being a unique and valuable individual in my own right, supplemented and complemented by my role as a mother. The first outline looked nothing like that.

I fell into the same patterns a lot of mothers and fathers do: everything becomes about the kids. But this isn't a parenting guide. Or at least it's not meant to be–it's about being a person and raising my kids to be good people, too.

I doubt James Madison ever considered his words on forming a new nation would be applied in quite this way but they truly do suit. He said: "all power should be derived from the people".

People. Not kids, not parents. PEOPLE.

Now bringing those democratic words into a family system metaphor invites questions like: *Do the kids we raise count as people? Should they have a portion of the power? Is it all one thing or is it situational?*

These are tough questions. My answers won't be the same as the next person; my answers aren't even always the same as Hubs' answers!

For me, I think the percentage of 'personhood' should ideally be 100% for adults and children have a percentage that increases as they mature.

2

More questions to follow:

What's the initial rate of personhood and how does the percentage increase? Is it a set amount per year, like a birthday present? Should my 11-year-old have a higher percentage of 'personhood' in the equation of decision making than my 6-year-old? How do their personalities and habits play into the percentage?

For me, the percentage of personhood for my boys is fluctuating, a daily–sometimes situational–calculation that's more of an art than a science. For instance, what haircut they choose is a situation where our boys have about 90% 'personhood' autonomy.

The last 10% remains as a guiding hand, allowing for me to insist we get haircuts (for hygiene reasons) and Hubs to veto bleaching/permanent hair dye (for safety reasons). I don't understand his reasoning there–I have my hair bleached and dyed purple every 3 months or so–but as his partner, I support him.

In other circumstances, the kids have a lower percentage of that autonomy, like when it comes to brushing their teeth. It's a battle five nights out of seven but it has to be done.

Leaving aside the ambiguity of personhood, let's define the other side of the equation: power. What is this thing Madison said should come from the people (and presumably for the good of the people) in the context of a family?

There are a lot of different definitions for the word power but what it really boils down to are two intertwined variables: physical capability and mental efficacy.

I have *power* if I have the combination of physical capability and mental efficacy to control my situation. That combination is transactional and situational.

It's an equation:

$$\text{Power} = \text{Physical Capability} + \text{Mental Efficacy}$$

Hear me out!

Take the movie Megamind. Both Megamind and Metro Man had 'power' at different points in the film. Metro Man had more physical capability, Megamind had more mental efficacy. Both hero and (sort of) villain shifted and changed their inputs of both variables to maintain (or regain) their power.

In real life, I'm much more like Megamind. I use mental efficacy to balance out fluctuations in my physical capability, because I have psoriatic arthritis.

My physical capabilities are limited in comparison to someone without arthritis. Especially on days when my hands decide they aren't going to hold on to things.

I don't lose my power just because I can't hold onto my phone! I have a PopSocket attached to the back that I can slide between my fingers to act as the grip I don't have that day. I've compensated for the change in my physical capability by using my mental efficacy!

My individual power equation would look like this:

$$100 \text{ (My Power)} = 40 \text{ (My Physical Capability)} + 60 \text{ (My Mental Efficacy)}$$

In a family, the equation grows and becomes more complicated. For our family, it looks like this:

$$\text{Power} = \{(\text{Hubs Physical} + \text{Mental}) + (\text{My Physical} + \text{Mental}) + [(\text{Mon Fills Physical} + \text{Mental})*\text{Peoplehood \%}] + [(\text{Mijo Physical} + \text{Mental})*\text{Peoplehood \%}]\} * X / Y$$

Now, I did add two unknown variables– X and Y– at the end to represent the multipliers and dividers of chaos. These are the events happening in school, the community, and the world that impact our family's estimation of power. We can't change those; we can only adjust our physical or mental stats in response.

As individuals, Hubs and I control our own parts of the equation. As parents, we can support and guide our children in controlling their parts of the equation.

We support their physical capabilities in a number of ways: good nutrition, therapy, regular doctor and dentist checkups, and reminders to look both ways before they cross the street. Normal, everyday stuff—

DON'T PICK UP THE DOG POOP! No, just–just put it down and go wash your hands. Right now. TOUCH NOTHING! I'll turn on the water—

Keeping two independent and curious young people physically safe is a full-time job, in and of itself.

Harder still is guiding kiddos in mental efficacy. Things like kindness, problem solving, time management, self-care, and resiliency.

These are difficult to measure and complicated to teach. It's an almost ineffable *feeling* we have to impart to them, so they feel confident in themselves and their own minds, so they know they are loved.

Safeguarding their physical capability while nurturing their mental efficacy is our goal as parents. We want our kids to feel safe and loved.

"You are safe and you are loved."

These two core statements are the foundation of our household. It may seem strange to some that these words need to be said, but they really do help. It may not end the tears or end the tantrum, but it's a powerful reminder to everyone–Hubs and I included–we are here for each other, no matter what.

Hubs and I started using the phrase with our first son, Mijo, when he was two, shortly after we first got him. Like any toddler, he had tantrums and fits.

His were perhaps more intense than other kids' tantrums. Mostly because he was living in a new house, with new adults, and didn't have the language skills yet to ask or understand why.

The words became a mantra for Hubs and I as we worked through how to help Mijo *feel* safe and loved.

6

I don't remember where I first heard this line, whether it was in a parenting book, a TV show, or from a therapist. I don't remember whether I heard the lines separately and combined them or they were a package deal from the start.

What I *do* remember is the first time Mijo said the words back to me.

It was January of 2023 and I'd been fired for the first time in my life. There was a lot that went into that dark situation but the basic facts are pretty easy to relate: I reported being sexually harassed to the CEO and HR, then three weeks later both me and the HR person were fired.

I was devastated. I came home and Hubs made me spaghetti for lunch while I worked up the courage to call Mommo and tell her. I managed to get the words out around my tears and–Mommo being Mommo– she hopped in the car and drove two hours to sit with me while I grieved.

Hubs picked Mijo up from school and brought him home. We didn't have Mon Fills yet so it was just Mijo that came bounding into the living room where I was sitting with Mommo. I tried to smile through my watery eyes as I explained to him why I was upset. He was silent for a few moments and then put his little hand on my shoulder.

"You're safe, you're loved."

I thanked him, hugged him, and sent him off to play Legos with Hubs. After Mommo left, I joined the Lego building. What felt like the worst day of my adult life did have a silver lining.

Perhaps the most obvious indicator Mijo has faith in those words is the fact he now brings up I was fired without an ounce of concern I might be upset.

He'll tell his friends, "My mom got fired." Then he'll move on like it's nothing more traumatic than a stubbed toe or a dropped snack. While I'm still processing the event two years later, each time he tells someone, it gets a little easier to smile or laugh.

Because I am safe and I am loved.

Of course, like with anything adult approved or parent promoted, there are times when the kids push back.

My oldest, Mon Fills, is a pre-tween. It's a minute-by-minute coin toss whether he is going to accept anything the parentals have to say.

He's also had a different journey in his twelve years of life. Safety and love were sporadic. His mom and dad struggle with addiction. Mon Fills has stayed with a number of different family members over the years. Before he came to our family, he lived with his dad's sister.

He never talks about his time there.

Sometimes when I tell him he is safe and loved, he dismisses me or flat-out snarls at me. And I get it. He's still settling into our family.

He's so used to bouncing around homes every year or two. Trust is at a premium. We are getting there, though.

As with all kids, he desperately wants to be loved. At first, he tested boundaries to see what it would take for us to stop loving him. Hubs and I were ill equipped in the beginning to understand how to help him.

Thank goodness for therapy! I have to send a huge thank you to all the therapists who have helped our family in the last few years.

Parenting is hard. Like super hard. But the rewards are more than worth it.

The progress toward acknowledging and voicing his love for us was slow going. He took an indirect approach at first, probably subconsciously worried about being rejected.

He came home from school one day, a few weeks into his French classes, absolutely fixated on learning how to say 'I love you' in French. We looked it up: 'Je t'aime'.

He started using it after saying goodnight at bedtime. Then he started using it when he was bouncing out of the car at school drop off. Now he uses it sporadically and interspersed with 'I love you' in English.

Progress!!!!!!

He's feeling love and feeling loved!

Safety is a tougher battle. The human race is biologically coded to acutely remember danger and trigger instinctual responses when similar circumstances occur.

All Hubs and I can do is remind Mon Fills and Mijo they are safe and try to actually keep them safe. Again, that's a tough battle.

Both my boys are very stubborn and are the types that have to learn the hard lessons for themselves. They are going to touch the hot plate even after being told it's a hot plate.

Where they differ is that Mijo will let go of the plate and acknowledge it hurt. Mon Fills will hold onto the plate tighter and insist it isn't that hot.

Not for nothing, but there is so much of me in Mijo and Mon Fills is so much like Hubs! They aren't our biological children but they are our kids, through and through.

People, Purpose, and New Perspectives

I love the beach.

The vastness of the ocean makes my anxieties feel small and quiets my mind. Thanks to the modern understanding and acceptance of mental health spectrums, anxiety is no longer dismissed or ignored. There's a name for it and a place for it in our social discussions.

We need to talk more about anxiety, because it is just as much a part of the human condition as love, shame, and imagination. Maybe it's a byproduct *of* our capacity to imagine love or shame as a possible outcome of our actions.

For me, my anxiety used to be about my purpose in the world. I was always worried I'd lead a small, meaningless, and lonely life. Another universal quality of humans–regardless of faith or creed, we all search for meaning in our life.

Novels, blockbuster movies, and even sometimes our weekly tabletop role playing game sessions all place importance on big acts of heroism and fantastical tales of legacy-creating events. Real life (thankfully) doesn't always have those circumstances.

Finding purpose and forging a legacy is more complicated than in the media we read and see. The reason is simple: truth is rarely as entertaining as a good story. I realized this while writing story of our tabletop adventures in novel form for our game runner, Smithy.

Our gaming family gets together every Saturday. Ish. Since 2019, we've been playing games, hanging out, and eating meals together when adulting responsibilities–and quarantines–allow.

The second campaign we played was set in a world Smithy created. The combination of an amazing world, phenomenal role playing by the group, and my own resonance with my character's search for purpose led me to write down everything that happened in the game.

It began as an idea to catalog a wonderful campaign for Smithy, a birthday gift to remind him he should be proud of himself. The first iterations were written like a journal from my character's perspective.

It had EVERYTHING we did from every session. Even the 'shopping episode' sessions where nothing important or serious happened. I was so proud of my little manuscript! A faithful recollection of all we'd gone through, a written account of the memories of my imaginary character.

I gave Smithy his present (several birthdays late) and we decided to publish it. Moving the story toward publishing, it was clear we couldn't keep everything.

Not every moment of every session was important to the character's journey. As much as I loved each 'argument' between my character and her overprotective grandpa, played by Grandar, not all of them needed a full scene and set dressing.

12

As much as we all loved the FOUR FULL SESSIONS our characters spent playing carnival games and goofing off in one of the cities we visited, I had to cut the two pie eating contests, the hammer throw competition, and the theater play.

For the good of the story, the full truth had to be trimmed.

We still ended up with three novel length books, but it was trimmed! We promise!

My character found purpose and meaning by the end, even though the reader only gets to see a fraction of her journey.

I've also found purpose and meaning.

If this were a novel of my journey, it would look a lot like being a parent *is* my purpose and the meaning of my life. In truth, it's more complicated and much more sustainable. Becoming a parent helped clear away the inconsequential things cluttering my perspective, blocking the long view of my journey.

Because kids ask questions.

A lot of questions.

Kids also have an innate ability to point out flaws in your logic. Especially when you didn't think there were any flaws in your logic!

"Why does the dog lick his butt?"

"Do I have to eat the broccoli?"

"If I were a giant velociraptor, could I jump really high?"

All their questions have to be answered, forcing me to distill my logic and beliefs into understandable, semi-coherent sentences. A beneficial byproduct of which is helping better understand my own self.

"Moooooommmmm, why do I have to be kind?"

Hmmm. Why do we have to be kind?

Well, the fact is, we don't *have* to be kind. I want my kids to be kind. I want them to *want* to be kind.

"Why, Mom?"

While I truly believe spreading kindness brings rewards throughout life–as in, karma comes for us all, so you better make sure it's positivity and goodness boomeranging back to you–that's not really very good logic to a pre-tween and 6-year-old.

So why be kind?

Going back to the basics of humanity–love and shame—I can see in my own psyche how kindness ties to the need for love and an aversion to shame. Except I don't want to teach my children with fear; fire and brimstone threats of consequences aren't my style.

I want to teach them that people matter, not consequences. Treating people with kindness is telling each individual they *matter*. The return dividends also include my kids feeling like they themselves matter.

"Because you matter, and so is your brother. So be kind to him! Kind words and kind voices, please!"

For so many years, I heard the idiom about everything changing when you have kids. I didn't give it much credence.

I do now.

Perhaps the idiom is flawed in that it makes it seem like a person is stationary except for the swirling change of parenthood. Like I'm suddenly standing on a hill surrounded by a swirling whirlwind of tornado debris.

In truth, it's my *perspective* that's changed.

I'm not suddenly standing in the middle of a whirlwind on unfamiliar ground. No. It's more like I'm finally seeing past the whirlwind, finally recognizing the landmarks and scenery around me.

It's all about perspective.

My personality, the core of who I am, is the same person I was, but my perspective is different now that I have kids.

If we think about perspective as a function of the power equation we discussed earlier, it's quite easy to see that perspective shifts go hand in hand with life events that shift the power equation.

A single adult, living alone has the general equation that encompasses their perspective of day-to-day life and the power they have to control it:

$$\text{Power} = \text{Physical Capability} + \text{Mental Efficacy}$$

Adding a roommate or romantic partner to the mix changes the equation, adding more variables. When two adults decide to combine lives, the general equation becomes the couple equation:

$$\text{Power} = (\text{Adult 1 Physical} + \text{Mental}) + (\text{Adult 2 Physical} + \text{Mental})$$

Each individual's personal perspective changes—or should change—to now include consideration of, compromises with, and concessions to their partner. Of my best friends since high school, two of them (the Expat and the Dutchess) have this equation as the basis for their household equation.

I say 'basis' because the complexity and variables involved in a two-person household make for myriad variations on the basic equation above. Expat and her boyfriend have different perspectives and variables added to their family equation than the Dutchess and her husband.

My other best friend from high school, Joylyn, has the same basic equation as me. Mom, Dad, and two kids. Her kids are much younger than mine, though, so the specifics of personhood percentages and the extra variables look very different from my family. Still, whether we birthed our children or found them along the way, our equation—our perspectives—have changed.

The other thing I don't like about that idiom is it makes it sound like having kids is a singularity, a unique and unprecedented event. Everything changes when you have kids, sure, but not *only* when you have kids.

It's good, normal, and healthy for a person's perspectives to change over the course of a lifetime. I'm sure as our family equation continues to change, so will our perspectives.

So why am I making this point here? Why is this most important after being safe and loved?

Because too many people are made to feel less than because their perspectives, their family equations, are different. Too many times, the very personhood of individuals is minimized.

Especially women.

Over lunch the other day, the Dutchess and I discussed the pain we feel every time we see someone make derogatory statements about women who don't give birth. The Dutchess doesn't have children and may never have children. I have two kids, but I didn't give birth to them.

The Dutchess is no less of a person. I am no less of a person. I am no less of a mother. The insidious, underlying belief that women only have value as mothers or grandmothers hurts.

It hurts me.

When I hear my own father repeating propaganda he's been fed about the rights of women in our society, it hurts me.

Last summer, our family took a last-minute road trip to visit my nephew, the Great American Beanpole. He was working in Indiana, it was his first time away from home, and he needed emotional support.

Mommo, being Mommo, saddled up the troops and off we went. Mommo, Daddo, my niece Betty Boop, Mijo, and me. All in the car, driving through rural Indiana.

We saw a sign about abortion. I didn't say anything, I was driving, and I don't talk about things like that with my dad.

Then he said something. I don't remember what it was, but it was offensive. To the point I knew I had to speak up. Not for me, but for Betty. She was fifteen years old, impressionable, and listening.

The last thing I wanted her to take away from the trip was that women aren't worthy of the same rights as men. Now, those aren't the words my dad was using, but that's what it boiled down to—a woman loses the right to her body once she is pregnant.

Nothing I said convinced Daddo to change his perspective or acknowledge that he, as a man, doesn't really have a dog in this race. That doesn't matter, though, because my words weren't for Daddo.

There's a nasty inclination to say I don't have a dog in the race, either—I can't get pregnant so will never have to face the decision of an abortion. Again, doesn't matter, because my words weren't for me.

My words were for Betty.

In the same way I saw my mother stand up for herself and for her autonomy over the years, I wanted to stand up for myself and for Betty. I hope when the day comes that Betty wants to stand up for herself, she'll think of me as a role model.

Carrying that desire forward–the desire to model firm convictions and respectful communication of opinions–into my role as a mother is perhaps the most important thing I can do. I have a responsibility to teach my sons we stand up for the human rights of every individual.

No matter what else I do in life, if I can instill in Mon Fills and Mijo that people deserve to be treated as people–regardless of their gender, or religion, or nationality, or fashion choices–then my legacy, my contribution to Republican Motherhood, will be realized.

Salsa, Serendipity, and Therapy

Life is crazy. There aren't words to describe the unexpected and often untidy surprises of life. When I think about how to make a difference in the world, it's easy to be overwhelmed by the sheer volume of unknown variables.

Considering the connections between different variables and the domino effects of interconnectivity...makes me want to take a nap.

Then I remember the lesson of the Mysteriously Appearing Salsa.

Mon Fills and Mijo are typical brothers. One moment they are playing a game they made up called Farting Chairs, and the next moment they are arguing about who the dog loves best.

One afternoon, driving them home from school, I heard them arguing in the back seat. The core of the argument seemed to be as follows:

"No, I didn't!"

"YES, YOU DID!"

"NU-UH!"

"YEAH-HUH!"

I was about to put an end to the yelling when I smelled salsa. A strong smell of salsa.

We pack our kids snacks for school, but never anything as messy as salsa! For obvious reasons, their snacks are pre-packaged, predominantly non-liquid, sauce-less things like goldfish, beef jerky, and popcorn.

So, of course, the salsa smell was out of place. The kids were still yelling and I began to hear the sounds of punching and kicking.

I whipped around, caught a momentary glance of hands flying and salsa EVERYWHERE. There was salsa on the boys, salsa on the seats, salsa on the back windshield.

Mysteriously appearing salsa everywhere!

Neither boy would admit to having the salsa but neither boy ratted the other out. Progress of a sort, I suppose.

No one really talks about how to effectively and efficiently get two salsa covered children out of the car and into the bathroom to get cleaned up. There was a lot of screeching, a lot of dogs licking, and more than a few messes to clean up along the way.

Not what I had planned for our chill time before homework.

I didn't get around to cleaning the car out. People who know me know the cars we have are cleaned approximately once a year. Sometimes more, sometimes less. I wasn't overly fussed about the salsa.

The next morning, when the boys complained about the smell, I just raised my eyebrows and invited them to clean up their own mess. I had no takers.

As unplanned as the original salsa incident had been, its domino effects were even more unpredictable.

A few days later, Hubs picked the boys up from school and by the time they got home, all three were in a mooooooooood.

Especially Hubs.

I was in the house, three pots on the stove, making dinner. The kids came in and I got them started on chores and homework.

Then I heard Hubs hollering from the garage. He was fixated on cleaning up the mess in the cars and was trying to tell Mon Fills to bring him a vacuum. I got the vacuum out for Mon Fills and rushed back to the stove.

More hollering from the garage ensued.

With a heavy sigh, I went back out to the garage. It was the wrong vacuum. According to Hubs. He told me so (at top volume) and then devolved into complaining about the mess in the cars and the salsa that, by then, resembled dried vomit.

I sent Mon Fills inside and asked Hubs to calm himself. He grumbled and grouched, then said he'd keep cleaning the cars if I'd handle things inside the house.

Cool, done, already handling it.

An hour later, homework was done, chores were done, and dinner was ready. In slouched Hubs from the garage, scowling and silent. His contributions to the family conversation were minimal and delivered in a disgruntled mumble. At one point, he disrespected me with a comment and I asked him to leave the table.

He did and while he was gone, I told myself he was in a mood and to be grateful he at least channeled his mood into cleaning out the car.

Not long after, I went to pack the boys' snacks for the next day. When I couldn't find Mijo's lunchbox, I asked Hubs.

"In the car," he told me petulantly. I was well on my way to being in a mood at that point so I didn't respond. I just stomped my way out to the car to get the damn lunchbo–

I stopped short, staring through the passenger side windows. The lunchbox was still on the floorboard. The salsa was still on the back windshield. My grandma's 1950's iron was still sitting in the front seat next to opened mail and a Sonic receipt.

As a reminder, I don't clean our cars very often but even I know when a car ain't clean. Those cars weren't clean.

I wanted to blow a gasket, but I waited for the boys to go to bed before asking Hubs, "What would you like to discuss first?"

In a tone.

I call it my Mommo tone because I get it from her. It's sharp and brittle, and–admittedly–kind of condescending. It's Hubs' warning he done fluffed up.

After our discussion, I took a shower and Hubs actually cleaned out the car. Sort of. He still didn't find Mijo's secret Pop-Tart stache or the open Chick-fil-a sauce container under the passenger side front seat.

Most of the salsa was gone, though, so I count it as a completed side quest.

The salsa was a spill too far for Hubs to live with that day but he was so dis-regulated he couldn't clean it up. It seemed obvious from the outside Hubs was going through a mental health moment at the time.

It was never really about the salsa, or the messy cars, or the correct vacuum. Hubs needed help but couldn't ask.

The salsa gave him the outlet to display his struggle, giving us the chance to bring the incident to our family therapist and get Hubs help.

Another shout out to our team of therapists. I can't say enough good things about therapy! Everyone should have a therapist.

Let me repeat that, louder this time: EVERYONE NEEDS A THERAPIST. I don't care how smart or well-balanced or 'fine' you think you are, get a therapist. If you wait until you 'need' it, you've waited too long.

My therapist helped me recognize the call for help that was the car cleaning incident. I will always be grateful to her and grateful for the Mysteriously Appearing Salsa. As ridiculous as it felt at the moment, it gave valuable dividends in the long run.

Finding the good in a situation, no matter how disruptive or devastating, is a foundational tenant of my personality. I haven't figured out if I can teach my boys this kind of positivity or resiliency or self-imposed delusion (whatever you want to call it), but I'm going to try!

Blood, Water, and the Love of Others

Returning to our patriotic analogy using the words of James Madison, we come to his wisdom on how power should be invested over time: "those entrusted with it should be kept in independence on the people, by a short duration of their appointments placed not in a few, but a number of hands."

Adjusting for language and applying known cultural norms, we can surmise Madison meant power over people should never be permanent nor invested in a single individual. We see that in politics with the separate branches of government and laws like the 25th Amendment.

In a family, I take Madison's words to be a companion quote to the idiom: "the blood of the covenant is thicker than the water of the womb". The expression is often truncated and warped into 'blood is thicker than water', which is the exact opposite of the original intent.

In evolutionary terms, I understand why focusing on blood bonds was important; until the modern era, humanity was in full survival mode as a species. Emphasizing blood bonds increased species survival rates.

Now, however, our species is the apex predator of our world. We no longer simply survive as a species, we are thriving. Individuals may still be facing survival uncertainty, but as a species, we're good. Thriving as a species changes the emphasis of where we invest our time, resources, and emotions.

Gone are the days when sticking with blood family was the best chance of living. In fact, most individuals who experience violence in their life do so at the hands of blood family. Domestic and familial violence–both physical and psychological abuse– is common regardless of what country or culture we examine.

I'm not qualified to understand all the whys and whatfors, but regardless of the combination of reasons, abuse is never okay. Up until the recent past, most people had few choices but to endure. Especially women.

It wasn't until the late 1970's that an American woman could take a loan from a bank without a man to co-sign!

Mommo was a single mom of two by the time the Equal Credit Opportunity Act was passed. It's wild to think about.

As much work as there still is to be done, I have to be incredibly grateful we've made it this far. I believe the next step in ensuring the freedom and equal rights of ALL persons is normalizing the idea of a chosen family.

Let's talk about what a chosen family is and is not.

Chosen family IS a family or network or village of people that choose to build and maintain close relationships. Sometimes, members of biological or blood families are also part of a person's chosen family. The important part is the choice, the covenant formed between people.

Consider a typical adult's closest and most important relationship: their intimate partner or spouse. This is the quintessential, foundational, most common example of chosen family. We choose our partner and form our own family.

Hubs and I chose each other, then over the years, we've added a whole host of family with chosen kids, grandparents, brothers, sisters, and more. We've also had to walk away from people because a chosen family is NOT permanent.

That statement has the potential to make a lot of individuals anxious. The idea of close, familial relationships being dynamic and transient sounds on the surface like a lack of security and support.

Nothing could be farther from the truth. Developing a large, diverse, and unique chosen family gives your life the resiliency to weather most situations. And the freedom to walk away when it's necessary. The beauty of chosen family is the choice to make a change.

Change is okay.

As individuals, we grow and change constantly. Is it any wonder the things and people most important to us when we are 18 change by the time we are 30? Our living situations, jobs, health, and physical appearance all change, why wouldn't our families change as well?

So often, we think of change as a negative, like we are losing something, but that's not always the case. My chosen family has changed drastically in the last decade. I've lost blood relations and chosen family members. I've also gained more than I could ever hope for: my kids.

Yes, there are painful points of loss. A friend of more than twelve years decided she didn't have room in her heart or her life for me—those were her words, not me being overly dramatic.

I had to sever contact with a blood relation who threatened my brother's livelihood. Each loss hurts but each loss is necessary for their well-being or for mine.

More than the losses, there have been unimaginable gains. My children are at the top of the list but are by no means the end. Dutchess, Joylyn, and Expat—my best friends since high school—have each brought a significant other into our family.

Hubs' best friend since middle school, a gentleman I refer to as his First Wife, brought his wife, Dex, and together they brought two beautiful children into this world and into our family.

Perhaps the most unexpected additions came from Hubs' tabletop gaming shop. He met and befriended first Grandar, then Smithy. Our gaming group has grown larger and closer, choosing to invest time and emotion in each other.

No matter how long or short a time our family stays together, I will always be grateful for this time we've had together.

Unlike blood relations, which are permanent and unalterable, a chosen family is a living system of continual decisions. The more we normalize the idea of choosing our family as opposed to blind loyalty to blood, the stronger, kinder, and more diverse our families will be.

None of this is to say a chosen family doesn't have its ups and downs, don't disagree or argue or hurt one another. We do. It happens. But the important part is how we recognize our mistakes then repair the relationships.

"How can we repair the relationship?"

Another common phrase in our household. I like it because it emphasizes the connection between people as opposed to the mistake of one or the other person. Putting our relationships front and center, even in times of disagreement or hurt, makes us stronger as a chosen family.

Repeated shout outs to our therapists for helping us develop the tools and language to keep our relationships at the forefront. With that mindset, it becomes very easy to choose kindness over being right or correct.

Hubs and Mon Fills struggle with the idea of disregarding correctness. They have very stark thought processes, task oriented with a premium on exactitude.

They aren't wrong. Their type of thinking is helpful in many aspects of life. But not when it comes to fostering relationships.

I'm not saying we should lie to the people we love, absolutely not! But there is a difference between being truthful and being correct.

Consider the scenario of field trip day. Driving the kids to school, Mon Fills knew Mijo had a field trip. Thankfully and gratefully, my contract work allows me to go on field trips with my boys. Mon Fills asked repeatedly if I would pick him up after the field trip a few hours earlier than normal.

I told him multiple times to plan on normal time, so he wasn't disappointed if the early pick up didn't happen.

"I make no promises, bud. Plan on normal time."

"What time is the field trip over?"

"I don't know the specific time; you need to plan on picking up like normal."

"They'll get back early, they always do. Pick me up early."

"I won't agree to that, you need to expect normal pick-up time."

Over and over again for the 30-minute drive to their school. His tasking brain wanted a singular, correct (in his view) answer. I was giving him truth but not correctness. Truthfully speaking, I wasn't giving him the WHOLE truth.

To be fully truthful and correct, I would have told him Mijo gets overstimulated on field trips and we often have to leave early.

In an enclosed space like the Science Museum, we can usually find a mother's room or breastfeeding room that's quiet and comfortable. Mijo will gravitate toward the less crowded spaces anyway, but having a sensory soothing space for breaks keeps him on the field trip longer.

The field trip of the day we are looking at was an outdoor family farm, set up for fall festival activities like hayrides. I'd never been there, so there were too many unknowns for me to guess at how long Mijo and I would be at the farm.

The field trip started out with there not being enough seats on the bus. I took Mijo in my car to make it easier on his teacher. After a 25-minute drive, Mijo and I found ourselves waiting in a line that stretched across the entire parking lot of the farm.

To pass the time, we played "I spy". Once inside, it got very crowded, very quickly. Thousands of kids and parents from every elementary school in a 50-mile radius.

While waiting for his class to get off the bus, Mijo found an empty stretch of pond shore and threw sticks into the water. Once we had his ticket from his teacher, he ignored all the kids in his class (especially all the little girls calling his name) and struck off for the open field with hay bales.

It wasn't an hour later, while eating an orange in the shade of the restroom barn, that Mijo asked to go home.

"I just want to drink water and see my dad," he said in a quiet, sad little voice. "I want to see my dad."

Believe it or not, his request represented huge gains in his ability to regulate himself. Six months before, I'd carried a screeching and scratching Mijo out of a field trip location. He has started recognizing himself when he doesn't like how an experience feels for him.

It wasn't even noon yet but we left. At that point, the utilitarian parent calculations of what is the most good for both boys looked something like this:

Best Outcome= (Time of Day * [Mon Fills Class Schedule + Known Tests * Classwork Due / Mental Fatigue] - (Mijo Mental/Emotional State * [Distance of Field Trip to School] - [Distance of Field Trip to Home)

We went home instead of driving the 25 minutes to pick up Mon Fills and then the additional 30 minutes home. Mon Fills would (and did) argue I wasn't correct in my calculations to leave him in school for the full day. I could have argued back and insisted on all the correct reasons why I did.

But for a 12-year-old kid that's upset and frustrated, what was correct didn't matter. Our relationship matters. I was fully prepared to respond from the relationship space when he walked through the door.

"You promised you'd pick me up early!"

"I absolutely did not! I told you to plan on normal time!"

Oops.

I messed up and I knew it. Big sigh to reset and:

"I'm sorry you misunderstood me this morning, bud. You're home now. Let's make dinner."

In the same way Mijo needed patience and understanding on Field Trip Day, I needed a lot of help and support on the day of his birthday party.

Because Mijo has a summer birthday, we offered him a deal: get Lego on your birthday and wait until the school year to throw your party.

Fast forward to fall and its finally time for his birthday party at the local skating rink. I made the invites, sent them out, got the party supplies, and was rolling into the party weekend feeling pretty good.

The party favors and gift bags wouldn't arrive until the Friday night before his Sunday afternoon party, but that was okay. I had it all under control.

We had a jam-packed family schedule the week before and it wasn't until we were driving home from visiting the G6 on Saturday night that I realized I hadn't ordered cupcakes. I had cupcake toppers but no cupcakes to put them on.

Anxiously putting together the party bags at 11pm, I started stressing about where I would get cupcakes before the 1p party. Logically, I know there were several places to get cupcakes or several ways to make cupcakes in the 14 hours I had.

But anxiety is not logical. It told me all the bakeries would be sold out and I'd have to rush home to bake cupcakes. Worse still, I'd have to buy canned frosting.

NNNNNOOOOOOOOOOOOOOO! I can't disgrace my family by serving canned frosting!

The spiral started fast and fierce, including some not so pleasant bathroom side effects. I was up and down all night until I gave up on rest at 5am.

I got up, did laundry, fed the animals, cleaned the litter box, picked up the house, and got dressed when I finally remembered Crest is open 24 hours.

Only the employees were there when I arrived. To my immense relief, there was a perfect batch of 24 cupcakes front and center in the display case at the bakery.

I was in line to check out when I remembered Mijo has a classmate that's allergic to all of the things. Racing past the stockers, I frantically searched for a good alternative.

I found a fruit tray with several different kinds of fruit, and decided it was time to get out of the grocery store before I ended up buying all the things in an anxious panic.

Back home, I found a new source of fixation: the gift bags.

What if more than 12 kids show up?

Tearing through the party supplies bin, I threw together a box of emergency party favors left over from past celebrations. I also grabbed some balloons, ribbon, and tape.

Around 7a, Hubs got up and promptly shepherded me back to bed where I cried for a solid half hour for no reason. Hubs soothed me and told me in no uncertain terms that he would be running the birthday party, not me.

I cried again, feeling like the worst mom in the whole world. Hubs reminded me over and over that I was safe and loved.

When the boys got up and around, I told them the truth, that I was having a hard anxiety day and crying a lot; I told them Mom may cry some more, but it wasn't their fault or anything they did wrong.

Mon Fills gave me a nod and returned to his breakfast. Mijo gave me a hug and ran off to find his All Might costume.

I also reached out to Third Mom and asked her to help Hubs. It wasn't fair to make him run his first kid's party solo. There's so much nuance and activity and multitasking that goes into it.

She readily agreed and I breathed a sigh of relief. I wasn't a functioning person but at least I could let go of some guilt.

More help was forthcoming from the gaming group. Stabby, New Girl, and Dex all reached out to ask how they could help with the party. More crying ensued as I explained to them I was in a bad way mentally.

They showed up early, helping decorate, get skates on kids, and generally just being supportive. Third Mom kept us on schedule and the family kept the guests engaged.

When it was time for cupcakes, Third Mom couldn't find the candles.

"I didn't get candles," I said out loud, already tearing up.

Smithy, bless his heart, looked right at me and said, "It's okay, we don't need candles."

Seeing the words on paper doesn't convey the calming and supportive way he said it, though. I didn't start crying, so that should tell you just how sweetly he spoke.

My chosen family came through for me and Hubs in a big way. I am beyond grateful for my chosen family and I'll strive every day to pay their kindness back and pay it forward.

That's how I want to practice Republican Motherhood.

The choices and decisions I make impact my bonds with my boys, Hubs, and all the amazing people in my chosen family. Big and small, each action has an effect.

I won't be perfect. I will mess up. But I will keep trying because my chosen family is worth it.

My relationships are a choice, not a chore.

My family is about bond, not blood.

My love is a decision, not a duty.

Dogs, Delays, and the Carolina Rescue

When I was a kid, one of my favorite VHS tapes we owned was *Rugrats Vacation*. I can't say why I liked it so much, all I remember now is a snippet of the titular song: "Vacation, all I ever wanted! Vacation, gotta get away!"

I love vacations! Who doesn't?!

Hubs would correct me and say I love to travel; he'd insist it's not the same as a vacation.

He's probably right. I'll try again.

I love to travel! Whenever the opportunity arises to visit a new place and see new things, I'm the first one on the bus.

Except I don't like bus tours because I want to plan my own itinerary and cram as much as I can into whatever time I have on my trip. To Hubs' eternal frustration, that usually means I spend *months* plotting routes, arranging sight-seeing or experience tours, and plugging hypotheticals into the Excel sheet I'm using for budget planning.

The daily itinerary always includes schedules, travel times, meal stops, and contingency plans. I like to plot out exactly what we are doing and when, then have multiple scenarios for how to adapt when the real world doesn't match my spreadsheet. For the most part, we make it through without much alteration.

You want to know what doesn't ever follow my timetables, spreadsheets, or expectations?

You guessed it.

Kids.

My intelligent, independent, stubborn little heathens are guaranteed to make changes to any plan or series of plans.

Traveling with kids meant I had to think about trips differently. Especially for *my* two kids.

Mon Fills has extremely high anxiety across the board–totally normal considering all he's gone through in his life. Traveling to new places and doing new things is hard for him. His anxiety manifests as 'turtling'–withdrawing, going non-verbal, etc.–or as aggression.

Mijo has diagnosed ADHD–which we term as Attention Different, (not deficit) Hyperactive Dude (not disorder). On top of that, he's an extremely extroverted empath, which basically means he gets charged up by being around people but he also reads and absorbs parts of their emotional state.

He's extremely good at reading and interpreting people's emotions, even though he himself doesn't have the mental function to name or process those emotions yet. Like when a storm chaser can 'smell' a tornado.

As a mom, it's my responsibility to help both my boys learn how to regulate and re-regulate themselves, with all of the bonus variables each of them bring to the table. As a travel lover, I want them to enjoy traveling, seeing new things, and meeting new people.

I'm the one that has to change my ways. Gone are the minute-by-minute plans and jam-packed itineraries. We went to Washington D.C. in the spring and had one big event or place each day. Everything else was fluid and happened as it needed to, including returning to the Airbnb in the early afternoon for some sensory reset time.

Growing up, returning to the hotel room or the cabin midday was unheard of; *we can sit on the couch at home* was the general feeling.

While I can only be grateful for the incredible experiences I had traveling with my parents, I'm trying to do something different with my boys. I want to give them more autonomy to listen to their bodies and minds, teach them how to communicate those needs, and show them we can still have fun while caring for our different travel mates.

In D.C., I started a Daily Dog Count as a way to get the boys to stop bickering in the Uber our first morning there. Little did I know they would take our Daily Dog Count and turn it into a highlight of the trip.

At the Mexican Embassy, we were in line for the Passport D.C. events and Mijo told another child about all the dogs we'd seen so far. Her father mentioned there was a park nearby where a lot of people walk their dogs. A few days later, our plan fell through so we headed to the park.

Not only did our dog count hit a trip-high 68, but one super nice lady let my boys play fetch with her dog (to Ghost's owner, thank you!) and I got to participate in a Smithsonian Institute research study about the dynamics of race and power. An amazing, unplanned experience driven by the boys' desire to pet all the dogs.

A less fun planned experience happened to the boys on the way home. I stayed on the East Coast for work. I dropped Hubs and the boys off at the airport at 7am on Wednesday, then drove from D.C. to New Jersey.

Real quick, fun fact: where we live in OKC, there's only one large commercial airport. It turns out, in D.C. there are TWO major airports. Hubs found out at the check in counter I'd dropped him and the kids off at the wrong one.

Oops.

One very expensive Uber ride later, they checked into the right airport and flew to New York to catch the connecting flight to OKC.

Or so they thought.

The flight was overbooked and in their infinite wisdom, the gate agent decided to kick the father traveling with two minor children off the airplane.

(Why? Why would you do that?)

Hours and hours of waiting in an airport later, they finally get on a flight to Charlotte to catch a different plane to Miami, then

OKC. The Miami flight fell through but they still had a shot to get to OKC through Charlotte.

Once they landed in Charlotte at 8p, they were exhausted. The flight to OKC didn't materialize but Hubs was heartened to hear there was a flight to DFW at 10p.

Back in Jersey, I started frantically searching for hotel rooms close to DFW and arranging for a family member to drive down in the morning to pick them up.

Hubs was ecstatic when they called for boarding. They made him check his carry on, the one that had his CPAP and medications, but he didn't make a fuss because they were finally going home.

Or so he thought.

An hour later, Hubs trudged back off the airplane, carrying a sleeping Mijo and trying his best to keep Mon Fills upright. Tornadoes in the area shut the airport down and they canceled all remaining flights for the day.

They refused to give him his carry-on back, so he was without his meds and CPAP. There were no rental cars left by the time they got to the rental area. Short of finding a family restroom to hole up in, Hubs was out of options.

Several states away, I scurried to get my boys somewhere safe to stay for the night. Expat lives in Charlotte with her significant other but they were in Ireland that week.

I called her anyway, hoping there was a spare key to their house hidden somewhere. No such luck but from Ireland, Expat started calling hotels in Charlotte.

The Dutchess works for a hotel chain. I called her and got her searching for a room as well. It was nearing 3am on the East Coast before we finally found a motel with an opening. It was only about–oh, 30 miles from the airport.

Another expensive Uber ride occurred but not before Hubs checked on rescheduling their flight. He was told the earliest would most likely be mid-morning.

On Friday.

With few other choices, I hopped in my rental car at 4a on Thursday and drove the 8 hours to Mooresville, North Carolina to rescue my boys! I got to them at noon. Hubs had slept for a few hours but not well because he didn't have his CPAP.

The man's life saving medicines and medical device were in that carry on and the airline wouldn't give it back! I was so angry I called the airline and lodged a complaint while I drove south. I'm still angry about it!

Anyway...reunited once again, we struck off for home. The kids slept a lot, and so did I, having been up from Wednesday morning through to noon on Thursday with no sleep. Poor Hubs was on his own to drive us home.

In a display of universal irony–or because of my scathing complaint– the carry-on beat us home, delivered to our front door several hours before we got there.

At the tender age of 6 and 11, the kids experienced all the frustration an airplane traveler may normally expect to encounter in a lifetime: wrong airport, overbooked flights, missed connections, delayed flights, weather cancellations, no rental cars available, sleeping in an airport, hotels with no vacancies, lost luggage (sort of), rescued by a family member, and an impromptu road trip.

They experienced it all in one 30-hour jaunt. Yikes.

We're going to Seoul, South Korea soon and the boys are going to have such a pleasant 26-hour travel time because it still won't be as long or frustrating as getting home from D.C.!

As for the itinerary in South Korea, each day is dedicated to a district of the city. I have a list of things to do in each area but the plan is to allow the boys to choose. The only 'must see' on my list is the animal cafe that has 40 different species of animals, including a golden raccoon!

I've tried to prepare the boys for their first international trip. I want them to know there may be times when we don't know what's going on. We don't speak the language, we don't know the city, and we'll have to rely on our wits, kindness, and resiliency.

We've stacked the deck a bit in our favor, inviting my nephew, the Great American Beanpole, along with us.

He's 25 and closer in age to me than I am to my brother, Cyclops. I was 10 when Great American Beanpole was born and 18 or so when he chose 'Great American Beanpole' for his wrestling name. We watched a lot of WWF/E back then.

We feel like a 3 to 2 ratio of adults to children will be a good thing in a giant foreign city like Seoul. It also gives Hubs and I a chance to take one evening to ourselves on the trip.

Fingers crossed all goes well!

Discipline, Consent, and How We Treat Each Other

The most recent addition to our chosen family–appropriately nicknamed 'New Girl' by our oldest–came into our life the same weekend Mon Fills moved into our house. She's only ever known us as a nuclear family of four.

I'll never forget how she described the parenting style we use. She called it 'a gentler approach'. I didn't have to ask her to explain, I knew what she meant.

Unlike the majority of parents we've had and known, Hubs and I don't use physical discipline. It's a total and complete departure from the parenting style our own parents used.

In my house growing up, discipline was doled out with fly swatters, belts, hands, and switches. For those who didn't grow up redneck, a switch is a stick, like a small branch from a tree or a bush.

"Go pick your switch."

A scary phrase to hear from your parents. Especially when you knew if you didn't pick a big enough switch, you'd be punished double.

I don't remember ever getting the switch but the threat was there. I did earn some belts, fly swatters, and a wooden spoon once. The most common tool was a hand, a spanking.

It was totally normal to me; if I messed up, I got hit. Parents, grandparents, and by extension, all adults in my life had the right to hurt me.

Remember what I said about kids clarifying your perspectives? As a parent now, I'm frankly horrified at the distilled lessons physical punishment taught:

1. Might makes right. If you are bigger and stronger, you can impose your will on others with physical intimidation and fear.
2. Your body is a weapon against you. It's okay for others to use your body against you, to make you do what they want.
3. Fighting is preferable to talking. Using physical force to get your way is easier and faster than using words.

My parents and Hubs' parents did the best they could with the knowledge they had at the time. I don't want to vilify them for their actions. In many ways, they improved so much over their own parents. It's only right I continue the progress forward.

I want my lessons to be things my kids can take forward into their adulthood. Physical discipline is not one of those things. As adults, that's called assault.

Or, if you feel that's too dramatic, consider a workplace situation. What would you do if your boss spanked you with their belt when you missed a deadline or messed up a client presentation?

What if your boss's boss came for a tour of your plant and smacked your hand with a wooden spoon if you messed up on the production line?

What would it feel like to have a coworker slap you upside the head with their palm for using their coffee creamer from the communal fridge?

You'd probably be really uncomfortable, angry, and demand they be fired!

So it didn't make sense for me to use those tactics with my kids. It doesn't teach them how to be functioning, positive contributors to the world.

I also believe physical discipline violates the primary, foundational promise we make to each other as a family: you are safe and you are loved.

Reflecting on the punishments of my youth, I didn't feel safe or loved when I was getting spanked. I vividly remember running from my grandpa as he pulled his belt off. I couldn't have been more than 5 (he died when I was 6), but I accurately remember the fear.

If I die tomorrow, I don't want fear to be one of the last things my kids remember about me. I want them to remember the love and laughs and goofiness.

Some may find it odd this chapter discusses discipline and consent. I deliberately chose to group them together because they are incredibly interconnected. Look back on the lessons physical discipline taught me.

Truly consider that in the context of body boundaries and consent.

I get what I want with force. I can use their body against them. Words are fine, but regardless if they agree, I will take what I want from them.

If I put it like this, does it start to sound really bad, almost like training abusers and rapists?

Respecting others' bodies starts with feeling like your own body autonomy is safe and secure. As a boy mom, I feel an extra responsibility to teach my sons about consent, about body autonomy and individual's human rights.

Of course, those are some lofty concepts to impart using negatives–or the lack of action. The absence of physical discipline isn't enough to solidify lessons of consent.

It's a foundation, rooted in self-worth and autonomy, but the application of those lessons out to others requires something more common and more demonstrable.

I chose dogs. Each dog we encounter, the boys must ask the owner for permission to pet the dog. They have to accept a "no" as gracefully as they accept a "yes". If they are allowed to pet the dog, one of them has to ask the owner the dog's name.

It's a small gesture but repeated hundreds–eventually thousands– of times. I'd like to think Desmond Tutu would consider it in line with his philosophy of spreading a little bit of good.

Conclusion

Here we are, at the end of this small treatise, having covered a few of the basics for my version of Republican Motherhood. There may be people who wonder why I bothered to publish this at all.

It's not a prolific work of genius. Quite the opposite. It's a messy, small, imperfect glance into my world. The word count or page length or concepts may not be to your liking.

I'm okay with that. I still wanted to share my world for two reasons.

First, looking at the creators I most admire–like Dolly Parton, Tupac, and Lin Manuel Miranda–they share their world and perspectives in unbelievable ways.

The amount of work each produces is staggering. I read somewhere that Tupac wrote so much music before his untimely death that his estate has released more than he was able to release in his lifetime.

Each of their stories contribute to our understanding of our history, culture, and social fabric. I hope to contribute, as well, with the small things I have to offer.

Second, there are so many times in life when simply knowing someone else is going through something similar really helps ground me mentally and emotionally. Like when I realized I wasn't the only girl who had hair growing on her toes.

Mommo's native blood means she has very little body hair and as my primary model of beauty as a girl, I was distressed that my body wasn't like hers. I was hairy like my dad and brothers.

Noooooooooo!!!!!

Absolutely devastating to an adolescent girl.

Until a friend told me she had hair on her toes, too. I was so relieved and so grateful she shared something I considered very embarrassing with me. It was a connection, a small thread of shared experience that contributed to the tapestry of my life.

If this small work gives another person a similar feeling, then I am well repaid for the time and effort of writing this book. Another small expression of good to give back on all the good that's happened to me.

Also by Dr. Amanda Wiles

Daughter of the Mountain
Heart of the Mountain

From Hells to Hollis
The Magi's Madame
The Assassin's Angel

Standalone
The Mad Science of HR
Republican Motherhood: A Disquisition on Life, Liberty, and
the Pursuit of Happiness